AN HISTORICAL VIGNETTE
of
OAK HILL
FAUQUIER COUNTY

Home of John Marshall
Chief Justice of the United States and
Native Son of Fauquier County

T. Triplett Russell and John K. Gott

HERITAGE BOOKS
2011

HERITAGE BOOKS
AN IMPRINT OF HERITAGE BOOKS, INC.

Books, CDs, and more—Worldwide

For our listing of thousands of titles see our website
at
www.HeritageBooks.com

Published 2011 by
HERITAGE BOOKS, INC.
Publishing Division
100 Railroad Ave. #104
Westminster, Maryland 21157

Copyright © 2000 T. Triplett Russell and John K. Gott

All rights reserved. No part of this book may be reproduced or transmitted in any form or by any means, electronic or mechanical, including photocopying, recording or by any information storage and retrieval system without written permission from the author, except for the inclusion of brief quotations in a review.

International Standard Book Numbers
Paperbound: 978-1-58549-591-7
Clothbound: 978-0-7884-8958-7

OAK HILL. From an early watercolor of both the 1773 (right) house and the 1818 (left front) house. The original watercolor was owned by Thomas Marshall Smith of Baltimore in 1916, and its present location is unknown.

MARY RANDOLPH KEITH MARSHALL (1737-1809). Daughter of the Rev. James Keith and Mary Isham Randolph, wife of Col. Thomas Marshall and mother of 15 children, one of whom was Chief Justice John Marshall.

Westmoreland Co., he moved to Germantown, Fauquier Co., and from there to "The Hollow" in Fauquier Co. in 1763. After the Revolution he moved to Ky., deeding "Oak Hill" (which he built in 1773) to his son, John Marshall.

"THE HOLLOW". Home of Col. Thomas Marshall, near present-day Markham, Fauquier Co. Built in 1763, this was the boyhood home of Chief Justice John Marshall. [Photo ca.1916]

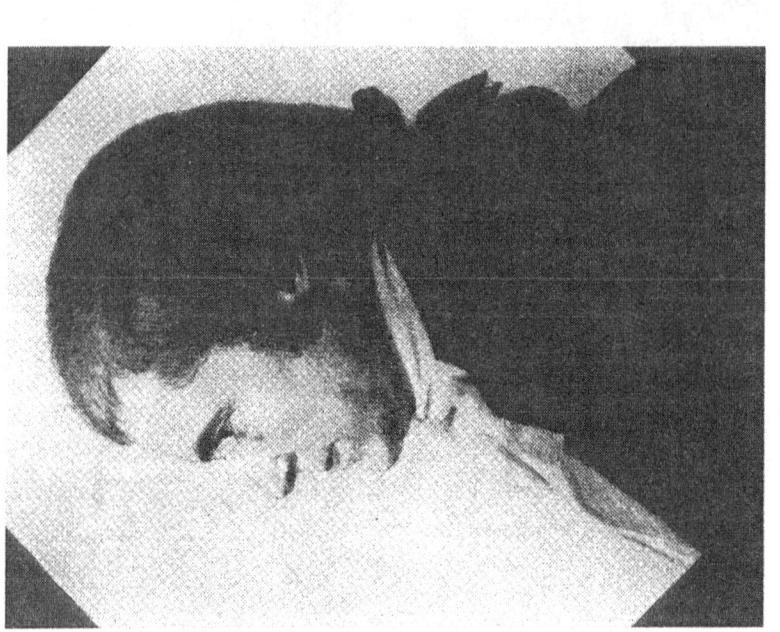

JOHN MARSHALL (1755-1835). Son of Col. Thomas Marshall and Mary R. (Keith) Marshall. Appointed Chief Justice of the United States in 1801. He gave "Oak Hill" to his son, Thomas Marshall.

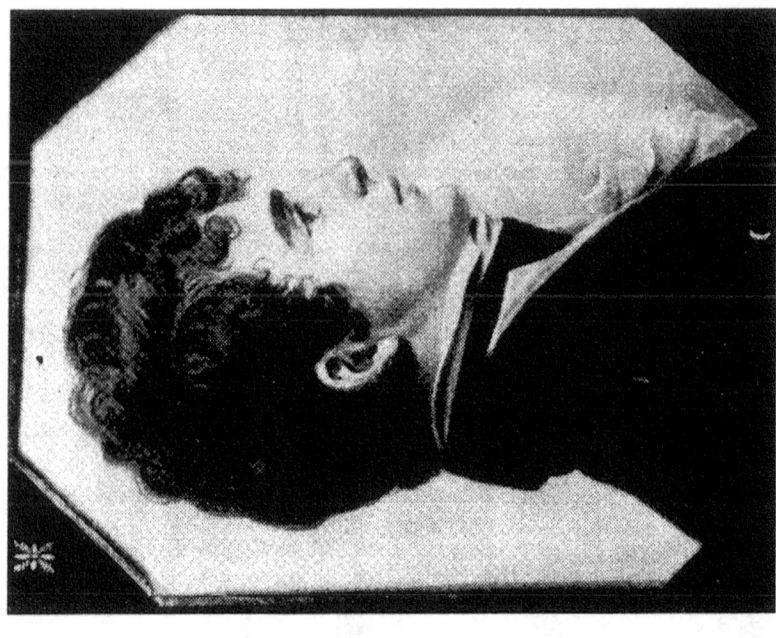

THOMAS MARSHALL (1784-1835). Son of Chief Justice John Marshall and Mary Willis (Ambler) Marshall. Thomas was given "Oak Hill" by his father, and built the "new house" in 1818. He was killed by a freak accident in Baltimore on his way to the death bed of his father in Philadelphia.

Foreword

This is the history of a house, of the land on which it was built, of those who built it, lived in it, and of the circumstances that made it as we see it today.

It is an historic house, partly because a famous man called it his home during much of his life, and also because the first house was built by a man who, were it not for the overshadowing greatness of his son, would be considered an important historical personage in his own right.

It is a house of great architectural interest. It is, in fact, two houses. One built in 1773, is a rare example of a Fauquier County farmhouse of the colonial period, left virtually unaltered by succeeding generations. The second house, built in 1818, is a sophisticated temple-form house of the Federal period. It, too, retains most of its original finely-detailed woodwork. It is noteworthy that the earlier house has not, as is so often the case, been replaced or absorbed by the later, larger house, but instead both have survived—affording an interesting comparison between the differing tastes of two generations, one in the middle of the eighteenth century and one of the early nineteenth century.

The history of the land extends back some forty years before the first house was built, and there we shall begin.

CHAPTER ONE

In the spring of 1732 Robert "King" Carter of "Corotoman" was reaching the end of his long and useful life. . He had been ailing for several years but, despite his duties as Virginia agent for the vast Fairfax Proprietary, granting land in the name of the Proprietor and managing his multiple and far--flung interests, Prospective purchasers of Fairfax land could not fail to note the old man's waning capabilities. Hastily they sought surveys of available up-country tracts to propose as suitable grants.

On the sixth of May 1732 came the blow from which he never recovered. On that day his son, Robert Carter of "Nomini," died. ... it has pleased the Almighty to take [him] from me in the flower of his age, to my great grief and confusion," he wrote.[1] Robert Carter, his favorite, the eldest son of his second marriage to Elizabeth Landon, was only thirty and was the only one of his sons to give promise of carrying on his work for the Proprietor. After his death Carter was no longer interested in the work that had occupied his time uninterruptedly for the past twelve years.

On the fifth of May 1732 Carter had signed a patent for 2,003 acres for his old friend James Ball of Lancaster County.[2] It was known as James Ball's "Horsepen Tract" and on it ultimately was planted the town of Marshall.

The following day, the day of his son's death, he signed another patent for James Ball. This was for 671 acres in a hollow between Ball's and Sugarloaf Mountains, called today 'The Cove.'[3] On the eighth of May there is a recorded grant of 579 acres within the present boundaries of Leeds Manor at a place known as Stillhouse Hollow.[4] It records no name, but it is supposed that it was intended for Captain James Ball. It bears the notation that it was left unsigned at Carter's death.

On May ninth there is record of a proposed grant to Charles Taylor of the County of Prince William for 1,700 acres at the North Cobbler Mountain and joining to the land surveyed for Captain James Ball.[5] With the foot of the North Cobbler on the northwest, it was a nearly square tract measuring about one and six-tenths miles on a side. The surveyor was John Warner, county surveyor of King George County, who did much of Carter's work in the upper reaches of King George and Stafford Counties. Not much is known of Charles Taylor except that he had, a year previously, patented a modest one hundred acres on Cedar Run northeast of Warrenton.

In the margin of the patent we read, "this deed was to have been granted to Charles Taylor but was left unsigned at Colonel Carter's death, so stands for nothing." There were many approved surveys in Carter's office, but there is no evidence that he signed any more patents before his death, 4 August 1732, at the age of sixty-nine.

Thomas, Sixth Lord Fairfax, Baron of Cameron in that part of Great Britain called Scotland and Lord Proprietor of the Northern Neck of Virginia, was thirty-nine when Carter died. While Carter lived he had shown a cool indifference to his vast holdings in Virginia in spite of Carter's urging that he pay some attention to his affairs. He seemed content with Carter's remission of quitrents, which seldom amounted to more than £400 each year. When he learned of Carter's death he realized with lightning speed that even this slender income would vanish unless he acted to replace him. After assuring himself that the Carter sons were unwilling to carry on their father's task, he considered several other choices before settling on his first cousin, William Fairfax, then Collector of Customs for Salem and Marblehead, Massachusetts. With the aid of his uncle, Bryan Fairfax, he secured William Fairfax's transfer to a similar post for Virginia's South Potomac, [Northern Neck], District.

William Fairfax's examination of Carter's books produced little except the understandable disarray during the last year of Carter's stewardship. The only thing that Fairfax could legitimately complain of were the enormous grants to Carter's younger children who were obviously not in a position to seat their estate for years to come. Lord Fairfax did not authorize the issuance of additional grants until he could see for himself how matters stood. Family affairs, including the death of his able younger brother Harry, kept him in England until February of 1735.

After several weeks of bad weather and worse food, he landed in Virginia in May and proceeded immediately to the house his cousin had rented in Westmoreland County. The land grant books were not reopened until the spring of 1737. Among the first grants recorded were two in the Bull Run Mountains comprising more than 5,600 acres for Mr. John Mercer of the County of Stafford.[6] It was explained that Mercer had obtained a warrant from "Colo. Carter, late agent, to survey a certain tract of wasteland, which survey was made by Mr. John Warner but not returned in time enough for a deed to be executed before the s^d agent's death."

In the summer of 1736 Fairfax, still unsure of the status of the proprietary grant, commissioned John Warner to survey all that land between the west boundaries of existing grants and the Rappahannock River at the mouth of Carter's Run and extending along that river to the Blue Ridge Mountains and along that ridge to Ashby's Bent.[7] This immense territory of 122,852 acres included within it three tracts already granted, "The Cove" and "Stillhouse Hollow", already mentioned, and a tract of 2,925 acres between Markham and Linden granted 13 December 1731 to Charles Burgess.[8] This patent was acquired on Burgess's death by Colonel William Aylett of "Coton" who displayed no interest in relinquishing his title.

The long and complicated survey of Leeds Manor was completed by John Warner 15 November 1736.[9] Accompanying it is a splendid map, which clearly shows the three grants in Leeds Manor east of the Blue Ridge.

It also shows Charles Taylor's grant at the foot of the North Cobbler. Once this tract was recorded Lord Fairfax felt no hesitancy about reopening the land grant books to all comers. Having arranged his affairs in Virginia as best he could under the circumstances and settled William Fairfax, his agent, at "Stanstead" on the Rappahannock above Falmouth, rented from Charles Carter, Lord Fairfax departed quietly for England in the summer of 1737. There he faced an even more formidable challenge, his battle with the Privy Council over the renewal of the proprietary charter itself.

Lord Fairfax had apparently instructed his agent against opening up new territory until the boundaries of the proprietary could be definitely determined but he continued confirming grants promised by Carter but never signed. He also made additional grants to Lord Fairfax, to his own sons and to friends, with the understanding that they would sign them over to members of the Fairfax family on demand. Among these was the grant to Charles Taylor who had died without heirs. On the 18th of November 1740 William Fairfax got around to dealing with Taylor's proposed grant.

When William Fairfax had come to Westmoreland County about 1734 looking for friends, one of the most important men thereabouts was Colonel Thomas Turner who lived at "Walsingham" on the Rappahannock River opposite Port Royal. Colonel Turner was county clerk and Burgess from King George County, colonel of militia and very wealthy. It is probable that Fairfax was welcome at

[opposite page]
OAK HILL. Plat of land grant to Maj. Harry Turner. He died in 1751, leaving the estate to his son, Thomas, who sold the tract to Col. Thomas Marshall in 1773.

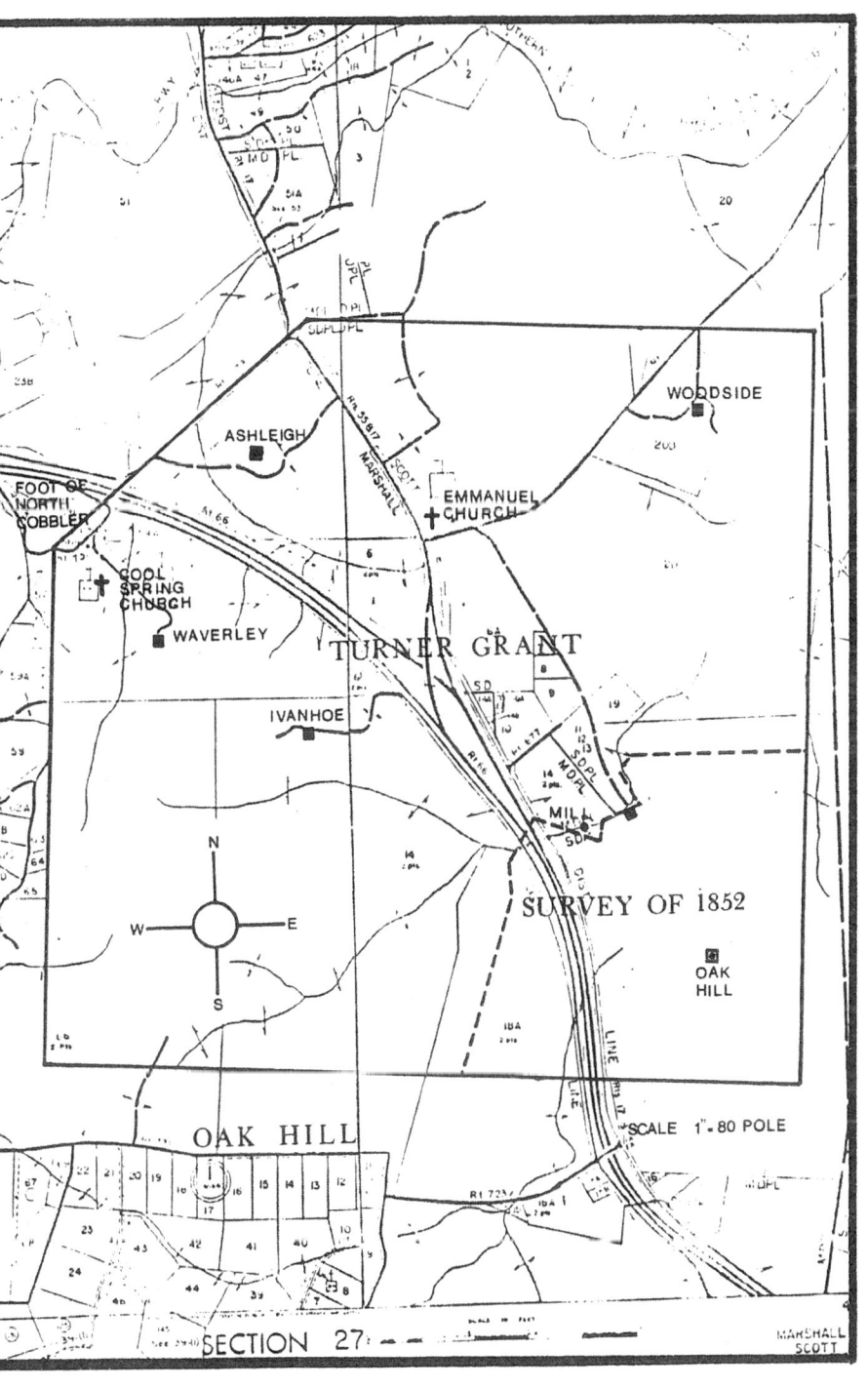

"Walsingham" and there met Colonel Turner's two sons, Major Harry Turner and Thomas Turner, Jr. In 1740, possibly as a token of his appreciation, Fairfax granted Taylor's 1,700 acres bordering Leeds Manor to Major Harry Turner, who was soon to marry Elizabeth Smith of "Smith's Mount," Westmoreland County.[10] She was the only daughter and heiress of Colonel Nicholas Smith, formerly a Burgess from King George County and a wealthy landowner. An additional 1,700 acres in this distant part of the proprietary cannot have meant much to Harry Turner who owned several large plantations nearer at hand. In fact it is doubtful that he ever ventured as far as the foot of the North Cobbler. He died in 1751 leaving his enormous estate to his only son, Thomas Turner, then about six years old.[11]

It is noted with interest that, in his last will dated 14 November 1751, Major Harry Turner left £20 sterling to Elizabeth Markham.

The third Thomas Turner (ca. 1745-1787) lived in the care of his grandfather until the latter's death in 1758. The land in Fauquier County was still unseated when he came of age in 1766 and shortly thereafter married Jane Fauntleroy of Richmond County. It is possible that he had established a quarter there a few slaves under an overseer before 1773 when he sold his Cobbler Mountain tract to Thomas Marshall for £912.10s.[12]

The sum may not have seemed like much to a man of Colonel Thomas Turner's wealth, but it represented a fortune to Captain Thomas Marshall. He also came from Westmoreland County and probably knew Colonel Turner, who was fifteen years his junior but certainly they moved in different circles. Thomas Marshall was born on Mattox Creek, Westmoreland County, 2 April 1730. He was the third child but eldest son of John Marshall "of the Forest" (ca. 1700- 1752) and his wife, Elizabeth Markham (ca. 1704-1775). John Marshall was a farmer who owned some 1,200 acres of land on Mattox Creek, most of it originally patented by John Washington and Nathaniel Pope and two hundred acres patented by himself in 1724.[13] He died in April 1752 when Thomas Marshall was twenty-two, leaving him two hundred acres of land long since worn out by too intensive cultivation. The younger Marshall promptly sold the two hundred acres, together with another hundred deeded him by his mother, to the churchwardens and vestrymen of Washington Parish for use as a glebe (a handy way of disposing of worthless land in those days). He then picked up his mother and as many of his brothers and sisters as chose to do so, and moved to Fauquier County.

He settled at Germantown, a rectangular tract of land on Licking Run, granted in 1720 to a group of German miners who had come to Virginia from Siegen, to work in Governor Spotswood's iron mines in Orange County.14 By the 1750s the Germans had largely deserted the place and the easternmost three lots containing 400 acres that had belonged to the Fishback and Hoffman families were available. Marshall may have built a house but it is more probable that some thing remained of the old Fishback house on the property in a place now pointed out as the site of John Marshall's birthplace.

In 1754, soon after arriving in Fauquier County, Thomas Marshall married Mary Randolph Keith, daughter of Parson James and Mary Isham (Randolph) Keith. Parson Keith was the Rector of Hamilton Parish and his glebe was not far from Germantown. Mary (Keith) Marshall is said to have been somewhat lacking in beauty, but whatever the lack she more than compensated by her superior education, remarkable health and willingness to work. Not to be overlooked is the fact that, through the Randolph family, she brought within the Marshall circle of kinfolk the most astonishing assortment of brilliant men ever derived from one family. Among them were Thomas Jefferson, Edmund Randolph, Richard Henry Lee, John Randolph of 'Roanoke', "Lighthorse Harry" Lee and his son, Robert Edward Lee.

Thomas Marshall quickly rose to a position of prominence in Fauquier. Having served as a deputy surveyor to Washington in Culpeper County, he obtained a license from William and Mary College and emerged in 1759 as Fauquier County's first county surveyor.[15] He soon obtained the job of collecting quitrents for Lord Fairfax in the same county. At the first court for Fauquier County, held a few miles from his house, 24 May

1759, he was sworn as Justice of the Peace and of the County Court in Chancery. In 1761 he was elected to the House of Burgesses and represented Fauquier County in that assemblage until 1767, when he was appointed sheriff of that county.[16]

On the 24th of September 1755 his eldest son, John, was born, followed in rapid succession by four more children: Elizabeth, (born 1756), Mary Ann (1757), Thomas (1761), and James Markham (1764). By 1765 Marshall had become disenchanted with the quality of his land on Licking Run and was ready to move elsewhere.

It has been mentioned earlier that the old Charles Burgess patent between Markham and Linden had come into the possession of Colonel William Aylett of "Coton." Aylett had, among other children, two daughters, Mary and Anne, who had married respectively Thomas Ludwell and Richard Henry Lee. In 1765 the Lees decided to subdivide the 2,925-acre Burgess grant into thirteen parcels for lease. Thomas Marshall took one of these parcels comprising 330 acres, on a small branch of Goose Creek near a spur of Naked Mountain.[17] In the lease, dated 12 October 1765, it is mentioned that the Marshalls were already living on the property. The annual rental was £5. Marshall had sold 250 acres of his Licking Run land 25 August 1765 to John Ariss, Gentleman, architect of 'North Wales' and other notable Virginia houses, for £250.[18]

On Goose Creek Marshall built a simple hall parlour frame house known today as 'The Hollow', in which he lived for eight years. During this time five more children were born: Judith (1766), William (1767), Charles (a twin of William), Lucy (1768) and Alexander Keith (1770). By 1773 there lived in this tiny house, (two rooms on the ground floor and a divided loft), Thomas Marshall, his wife, his mother, ten children and, amazingly, a Scottish tutor, the Rev. James Thomson, rector of Leeds Parish, who was employed to teach the older children. John Marshall, the future Chief Justice, was then sixteen.

A larger house was certainly called for, but Marshall was loath to invest his savings on 330 acres of leased land. Accordingly, Thomas Marshall shopped around for a more suitable tract of land. It is not known how he came upon 1,700 acres of prime land bordering on Leeds Manor below the North Cobbler owned but unseated by Colonel Thomas Turner of King George County. (Could the mysterious bequest in Harry Turner's will be a clue?) Marshall sold his lease on Goose Creek 11 September 1773 to John Webb of Northumberland County for £200, and concluded negotiations with Colonel Turner.[19] The deed from Turner to Marshall dated 1 January 1773, called for the payment of £912.10s. a huge sum for a man in Marshall's position.[20] His sheriff's bond for the collection of taxes in Fauquier County in 1769 was only thirty thousand pounds of tobacco, or about £150.

Marshall sited his house in a grove of oaks on a low hill near the southeast corner of his tract, which he called 'Oak Hill', or, in his will, 'The Oaks" It was not a large house (32' 3" x 30' 2") but in every respect it was vastly superior to the old house on Goose Creek.

It was built of frame on a stone foundation, with clapboard siding and massive brick chimneys on the north and south ends. The ground floor was divided into four rooms of unequal size, each with a fireplace. Under the steeply pitched roof with three narrow dormers were three rooms of which the largest had its own fireplace. There is a separate stair hall in which the stair, built like a box stair, (steep and with winders at the bottom), nevertheless has open treads with bracketed ends and a cherry handrail with turned balusters in the then current tidewater style.

The most outstanding feature of the first house built at 'Oak Hill' is its superb finish both inside and out, a good deal of which remains intact. Whereas finishes at 'The Hollow' were crude, even primitive, "Oak Hill" is sophisticated in the best English fashion. On the exterior the beaded siding, nine-over-nine sash with slender muntins, the simple cornice and handsome brick chimneys, all show quality workmanship. The north chimney, laid in Flemish bond with glazed headers in an elaborate pattern, is one of the finest in northern Virginia.[21] On the interior the paneling of the southwest parlour, with a denticulated cornice and an overmantel flanked by fluted pilasters, is similarly exceptional. The beautiful mantel in the northeast room, probably the Marshall's bedroom, or dining room, has reeded pilasters and decoration on the frieze in the manner of Robert Adam. Whence came all this refinement?

The answer may be quite simple. Marshall may have picked up a great amount of architectural knowledge from John Ariss, and what appears in the record to have been a casual connection may have been considerably more than that. It is in fact possible that John Ariss himself designed the first house at "Oak Hill". The stylistic similarity is striking. The house is little smaller than "Kenmore" in Fredericksburg, (27' x 35') and has a remarkably similar plan.[22] It was probably originally entered from the east into the stair hall, beyond which was the drawing room or southwest parlour. "Kenmore", attributed to Ariss, has the same arrangement. John Ariss was the only architect living in Fauquier County at the time capable of work of this quality. He was working at "North Wales" at the time, though "North Wales" would not be finished until after the Revolution. There will be later evidence of Ariss's handiwork.

As "Oak Hill" has always been a working farm, at least some of the existing outbuildings must be presumed to date from 1773. Just eighteen yards from the east wall of the original house is a straight line of outbuildings including a kitchen, slave quarters, a smoke house and other miscellaneous frame amenities. The kitchen and slave quarters are of particular interest as the most likely buildings to have been built along with the house. They are exactly the same length (32 feet), frame, on stone foundations with one solid brick chimney at the north end of each. The kitchen has three bays, one of which was probably the cook's room.

The nearly identical slave quarters also have three bays. Both buildings are one storey with lofts above. The log smoke or meat house between them is interesting, but probably belongs to the early part of the nineteenth century.[23] Other outbuildings include a stone spring house, a schoolhouse and various barns. The spring house may also be contemporary with the original house, but the original barns have apparently been replaced.

The construction was probably accomplished by a local carpenter with the assistance of Marshall's slaves and older sons. Finished details such as paneling, mantels, stair parts and window sash were probably fabricated in Fredericksburg where such facilities existed, as we know from the ledgers of William Allason, a Falmouth merchant, for whom "North Wales" was built. John Ariss would have known where such material was available. Since his appearance in Virginia in 1751, he had had wide experience in the lower part of the Northern Neck.

LIEUT.-COL. THOMAS MARSHALL

COL. THOMAS MARSHALL, JR., CSA (1826-1864). Son of Thomas Marshall and grandson of Chief Justice John Marshall. He purchased "Oak Hill" from his brother, John, and was the last of the Marshall to own the estate.

CHAPTER TWO

   John Marshall lived for three years at "Oak Hill" before he, with his father, joined the Culpeper Minute Men in the summer of 1775. His father was elected Major, he Lieutenant. During the past three years they had been preparing for military service. When he was fourteen John Marshall had been sent back to Westmoreland County for a year's schooling under the Reverend Archibald Campbell, Rector of Washington Parish. That and the tutelage of the Reverend James Thomson had given him a basic classical education at the end of which he was reading Livy and Horace in the original Latin. Somewhere along the line he must have picked up a copy of Blackstone's Commentaries, which turned his attention toward the law. That is all the formal education he had except as noted later, but it was considerably more than most Virginians of his time.

   The years before the war was a period of growth for John Marshall in other ways as well. Biographers have leaned over backward, in the American tradition, to picture him as an uneducated rustic, born in a log cabin, clad in homespun, doggedly defending the frontier. Nothing could be farther from the truth. The Germantown house, whoever built it, was not a log cabin; as such construction had not found its way to Virginia east of the Blue Ridge in 1755. As Burgess, Thomas Marshall made frequent trips to Williamsburg by way of Fredericksburg, and we may be sure that his son dressed as suited his station.[1] There had been no Indians in Fauquier since Spotswood's treaty with the Iroquois at Albany in 1722. It is not necessary in this history to give a detailed account of the military careers of Thomas Marshall or of his sons. It suffices to say that the Marshalls were good soldiers. Colonel Thomas Marshall commanded the Third Virginia Regiment in the Continental Line. As a lieutenant in the same regiment John Marshall served with distinction. His concern for the welfare of his men was especially noteworthy. During the terrible winter at Valley Forge he was one of few officers who refused to return to Virginia where many of his contemporaries were enjoying the comforts of home. From "Oak Hill" his two younger brothers, Thomas, Jr. and James Markham, also joined the service. It is just as well as, between 1773 and 1781, five more children were born to Colonel Thomas and Mary (Keith) Marshall: Louis in 1773, Susan Tarleton (1774), Charlotte (1777), Jane (1779) and Ann (1781).

Colonel Thomas Marshall was also at Valley Forge during the first weeks of the encampment. About the middle-of January he left for Virginia to take command of the newly raised State Artillery Regiment. About the same time John was made Captain/Lieutenant, a rather curious rank, and Thomas Marshall, Jr., aged seventeen, was commissioned captain in a Virginia state regiment.

The early spring of 1780 found the young Captain/Lieutenant "supernumerary." The company he had raised had long since evaporated through expiration of enlistments and battlefield casualties. Seeking a new command he joined his father in Yorktown. To while away the time he traveled the twelve miles from Yorktown to Williamsburg to attend the law lectures of George Wythe, the celebrated attorney, for about six weeks. This was the only formal education in law that the future Chief Justice ever had. He must have absorbed some of it, but law was by no means the only thing on his mind. His law notes are positively festooned with the name "Polly Ambler" in various forms.

Mary Willis Ambler was the daughter of Jacquelin and Rebecca (Burwell) Ambler of Yorktown. Her mother, in her younger days, had been courted by John Marshall's impecunious, red-headed cousin, Thomas Jefferson Instead she had married a wealthy Yorktown businessman, Jacquelin Ambler, who was the King's collector of customs in the Port of Yorktown. The war had reduced Ambler's fortune considerably so that they were living in a small town house in Yorktown adjoining the headquarters of Colonel Thomas Marshall. In the summer of 1780 she was fourteen and John Marshall twenty-five. For her, he decided he would wait.

He returned to "Oak Hill" in the summer of 1780, believing himself ready to practice law. Accordingly 28 August 1780 he presented himself at the county courthouse and produced a license signed by Governor Thomas Jefferson allowing him to practice law and was thereby admitted to the bar in Fauquier County. [2] He found "Oak Hill" in a run-down state, as might have been expected, but had not the means to make repairs. In the autumn he decided to be inoculated against smallpox, which had possibly caused more deaths in the American army during the Revolution than had the British. For that he had to go to Philadelphia, but transportation presented no problem. He walked!

Meanwhile in Yorktown, Colonel Thomas Marshall had given long and serious thought to the future of his family once the war was over. In the summer of 1780 he and a group of fellow officers visited Kentucky. Here, in this new and exhilarating climate he saw his future unfold. He resolved to return as soon as possible. That Kentucky was the logical area in which Virginia land bounties for service in the Revolution might be honored, was already a subject of wide speculation. On returning to Virginia Colonel Marshall set about winding up his affairs and preparing for a move to Kentucky. In Fauquier County Marshall appeared to be a rich man. He owned 1,700 acres of land, twenty-two slaves, horses and cattle. But the men had not been home for years to work the land and prices and taxes were high. He asked his old friend George Washington to help him out by buying part of "Oak Hill", but Washington was in much the same position and was forced to decline. Finally, 28 March 1780, he was able to sell one thousand acres at the northwest side of the "Oak Hill" tract to Thomas Massey of Frederick County for £30,000.[3] The land had not increased in value since its purchase seven years before. The difference was in inflation and the depreciation of paper currency.

In Fauquier County John Marshall was deep in politics. In the autumn of 1782 he was elected to the House of Delegates from Fauquier County. This honor helped his career in law and also brought him again to the side of the lovely, fragile Miss Ambler. Her father was well on his way toward financial recovery and was now treasurer of the Commonwealth, although, he ruefully admitted, there was little money in the treasury. Marshall had not been in Richmond two months when he was married. The event took place in Hanover County at the home of Mary's cousin, John Ambler, [3] January 1783. By his own account the bridegroom, after having paid the minister, "had but one solitary guinea left."

At the time of the wedding Colonel Thomas Marshall's plans to move to Kentucky were progressing satisfactorily. He gave his son a Negro and three horses as wedding presents. He had been appointed county surveyor for Fayette County, one of three enormous counties into which Kentucky (then still a part of Virginia) had been divided. His own holdings in Kentucky which included his own and his sons' bounty warrants, was increased by the purchase of other warrants of Revolutionary War veterans who were un-willing or unable to emigrate and needed ready cash. He had already opened a surveyor's office in Kentucky the previous November.[4] He was now preparing to take his wife, younger children, slaves, horses and cattle on that perilous journey in flatboats down the Ohio River.

In the autumn of 1783, after a hair-raising journey, they had reached their goal.

So ends Colonel Thomas Marshall's direct connection with "Oak Hill." He died 22 June 1802 leaving an immense landed estate. Two years before his death he and his wife had gone to live with their son Thomas at "The Hill", Washington, Mason County, Kentucky. Mary Randolph (Keith) Marshall survived him seven years. Over her grave her singularly ungallant son raised a stone inscribed:

Marshall
Mary Randolph Keith
1737-1809
She was good, not brilliant; useful, not ornamental
and the mother of 15 children.

From Kentucky, to be recorded in Fauquier County, 16 March 1785, came the following deed, quoted in part:[5]

This Indenture between Thomas Marshall of the Parish of Leeds, Fauquier County and John Marshall of the same - - for five shillings and love and natural affection for the said John.... that tract.... purchased from Thomas Turner, Esq., then of the County of King George, now Westmoreland at the North Cobbler Mountain.. containing 1,824 acres except 1,000 acres sold by the said Thomas Marshall and conveyed to Thomas Massey of Frederick County...

The surplus 124 acres is not accounted for, nor is the fact that neither party was then living in Fauquier County. Possibly they still considered Fauquier County home, whether or not they really lived there. John Marshall and his wife visited Oak Hill during the summer of 1783.[6] John's oldest sister, Elizabeth, was keeping house for his brother Thomas and whoever else of the Marshalls as chanced to drop by. Polly was rather overwhelmed by the boisterous Marshall clan and returned to their rented house in Richmond with some relief. There, 21 July 1784, their oldest son, Thomas, was born. A daughter, born in 1786, died at the age of six. The second son, Jaquelin Ambler Marshall, was born 3 December 1787.

Marshall's law practice was an immense success from the beginning. His glittering array of family connections and powerful friends, coupled with a real dearth of trained lawyers in the capital assured that. His father's position in Kentucky made him particularly equipped to handle pension claims and land bounty disputes. The number of cases he had in progress in 1786 made him a leading member of the Virginia bar. in 1785 he declined to run for a seat in the House of Delegates from Fauquier, realizing that his work in Richmond was enough to keep him fully occupied. He refused to accept cases from Fauquier County except those of his own family. Even those kept him running back and forth from Richmond to Warrenton at frequent intervals. In the summer Polly accompanied him.

There was, however, one client whose Fauquier County interests could not be ignored. He was the Reverend Denny Martin, heir to Thomas, Sixth Lord Fairfax, who had died 9 December 1781.[7] Under the terms of Lord Fairfax's will, his nephew Denny Martin, provided that he "procure an Act of Parliament ... to take upon him the name of Fairfax and coat of arms," inherited the vast estate. In October of 1784, following the confirmation of the Treaty of Paris, Martin came to Virginia to find out the status of his inheritance. Admittedly he was an enemy alien but just as certainly he was the legal heir of Lord Fairfax, entitled to unappropriated lands and uncollected quitrents. For advice he sought the aging Gabriel Jones, "the Valley lawyer," and the young and rising John Marshall. Marshall advised him to procure the name change post-haste, and he would deal with the rest. In 1786 he filed caveats against all grants by the Virginia government in the Northern Neck territory. He asserted title to Leeds and other manor lands as well as other unappropriated land in the former proprietary.[8]

Fairfax visited his brother, Colonel Thomas Bryan Martin, at "Greenway Court" during his stay in Virginia and, on the way, may have stopped at "Oak Hill." If so, he may have met there one Rawleigh Colston, Virginia-born but newly returned from Santo Domingo where he had made a considerable fortune. Rawleigh Colston and Elizabeth Marshall, John's oldest sister, were married 15 October 1785 at John's house in Richmond.

It is not known when John Marshall, his brother James Markham Marshall, and Rawleigh Colston decided to combine their fortunes and attempt the purchase of Leeds Manor, but it was probably ten years after Denny Martin Fairfax had returned to England.

Between 1788 and 1792 Polly Marshall had a series of losses that would have "shaken the frame" of a much hardier woman. In 1789 a son was born who died before he could be given a name. In 1788 there was another daughter, probably stillborn. A son born in February 1792 died in August, his death coinciding with that of her older daughter. The ordeal intensified the nervous affliction that had plagued her since her marriage and she seems to have acquired a form of anemia that completely sapped her strength. In 1790 John Marshall had a handsome brick house built for her but the noise of construction, even at a distance, nearly drove her mad.

In the autumn of 1788 and spring of 1789 Richmond was thronged with visitors attending the convention for the ratification of the Constitution. The demands made on Marshall's time during that period were enormous. Ratification came 4 March 1789. Not long after the new President, George Washington, asked Marshall to accept the office of Attorney General of the Commonwealth of Virginia. Marshall declined. He said he was too busy.[9]

Thomas Marshall, Jr., married 11 September 1783, Susannah Adams and, in 1790, departed for Kentucky by the same route his father had taken, down the Ohio River.

For a while "Oak Hill" was unoccupied even in summer, for Polly was too ill to make the journey. She did not see it again until the summer of 1794, when an unusually hot spell and the dirt and noise of Richmond drove her to the mountains.

At "Oak Hill" and in Richmond four ambitious Americans met in the autumn and winter of 1793 to discuss a dazzling project proposed by John Marshall, nothing less than the purchase of Leeds Manor from the Fairfax heirs. John Marshall had a lucrative law practice and great financial courage. James Markham as European commercial agent for the cities of Charleston, New York and Boston, had unlimited prospects. Rawleigh Colston had wisely invested the fortune he had made in the West Indies. The fourth member of the proposed syndicate, Governor Henry ("Lighthorse Harry') Lee, had a store of expansive plans but, unfortunately, no money. Eventually Colston had to buy him out.

They proposed to offer, in May 1793, the sum of £ 14,000 for the property. However, the offer was not equivalent to a sale. First, the claims of the Commonwealth of Virginia must be settled and, important, the money raised. John did not think that the Virginia claims would stand in the way. James Markham Marshall did not think that raising the money would present a problem. By a rather curious coincidence he was engaged to marry Hester Morris, only daughter of Robert and Mary (White) Morris of Philadelphia. Robert Morris was a fabulously rich banker and financier who did, in fact, help finance the Revolutionary army. He was interested in land speculation and could be counted on to aid his future son-in-law. James Markham Marshall married Hester Morris at her father's lavish house in Philadelphia, 9 April 1795. Alas, it was then revealed that Robert Morris had lost his vast fortune in speculating on land in western New York and was, in fact, teetering on the edge of bankruptcy. On the 18th of October 1795 young Marshall and his bride sailed for England to see Fairfax and seek another source for funds.

  The Marshalls omitted their usual visit to "Oak Hill" during the summer of 1795 as Polly was expecting another child. She was afraid to be away from her Richmond doctors. On the 17th of September a fine girl was born, promptly named Mary. She would outlive both her parents. Early in 1796 Marshall left for Philadelphia to make his first appearance before the Supreme Court of the United States. He was home again in March and that summer Polly and the children spent at "Oak Hill." She was to have three more children, John, born 15 January 1798; James Keith, born 13 February 1800; and Edward Carrington, born 13 January 1805.

  In February 1797 James Markham Marshall, in Holland, succeeded in raising more than £7,000 from a Dutch banker named Hottenguer. It was done on the European credit of Robert Morris and was promptly applied as part payment for Leeds Manor and other Fairfax manors in Virginia. Denny Martin Fairfax gave title the next August to the other manors, but withheld title to Leeds Manor until full payment should be made. [10]

In the summer of 1797 John Marshall was sent to France with General Charles Cotesworth Pinckney, Secretary of State, and Elbridge Gerry of Massachusetts to sort out the troublesome X. Y. Z. affair with the haughty French foreign minister, Charles Maurice, Compt de Talleyrand-Perigord. He was in France until 17 June 1798, almost exactly a year after his departure, and six months after the birth of his son John. Then, in February, Polly's father died. Polly was prostrate. She fled to the Colstons in Winchester leaving her infant son in Richmond. When John Marshall returned to Philadelphia he learned of Polly's collapse and that Robert Morris was in debtors' prison where his wife had to pay his board.

On the twenty-fourth of June, Marshall was on his way to Winchester. Strapped around his waist were two thousand dollars paid him on account by the State Department. Full possession of Leeds Manor was moving closer. Marshall spent six weeks with his wife at the Colstons, also visiting the Virginia mineral springs, including Fauquier's White Sulphur. He returned to Richmond in early August. He reported to Polly in Winchester 18 August 1798 that he had found their three year old daughter "fascinating" and their son John small and weakly "but by no means an ugly child." The two older boys, Thomas, aged fourteen, and Jaquelin, eleven, were not at home. [11]

Soon afterwards he received a summons from General Washington at "Mount Vernon".

Washington, in no uncertain terms informed him that it was his duty to run for a congressional seat from Virginia. With extreme reluctance, Marshall consented, although he feared that neglect of his law practice during a long campaign might cost him Leeds Manor. This concern was somewhat alleviated when the State Department paid him $14,463.17 as the balance due for his French mission, which he applied largely to payment on the Fairfax land. He then rode happily to Fredericksburg to meet Polly.

The campaign was a bitter one. His opponent John Clopton was not formidable, but behind him was the sinister hand of Thomas Jefferson, who hated Marshall with venom. Despite Jefferson, Marshall won with a narrow margin on the most bloody election day Richmond had ever known (June 1799). In August Marshall rode to Kentucky to pay a long-postponed visit to his father at "Buckpond". It was then or never. Colonel Thomas Marshall was deeding "Buckpond" to his son Louis Marshall and going to live with his son Thomas at "The Hill" in Washington County. As for John, he expected that the Sixth Congress of the United States would occupy his energies for some years to come.

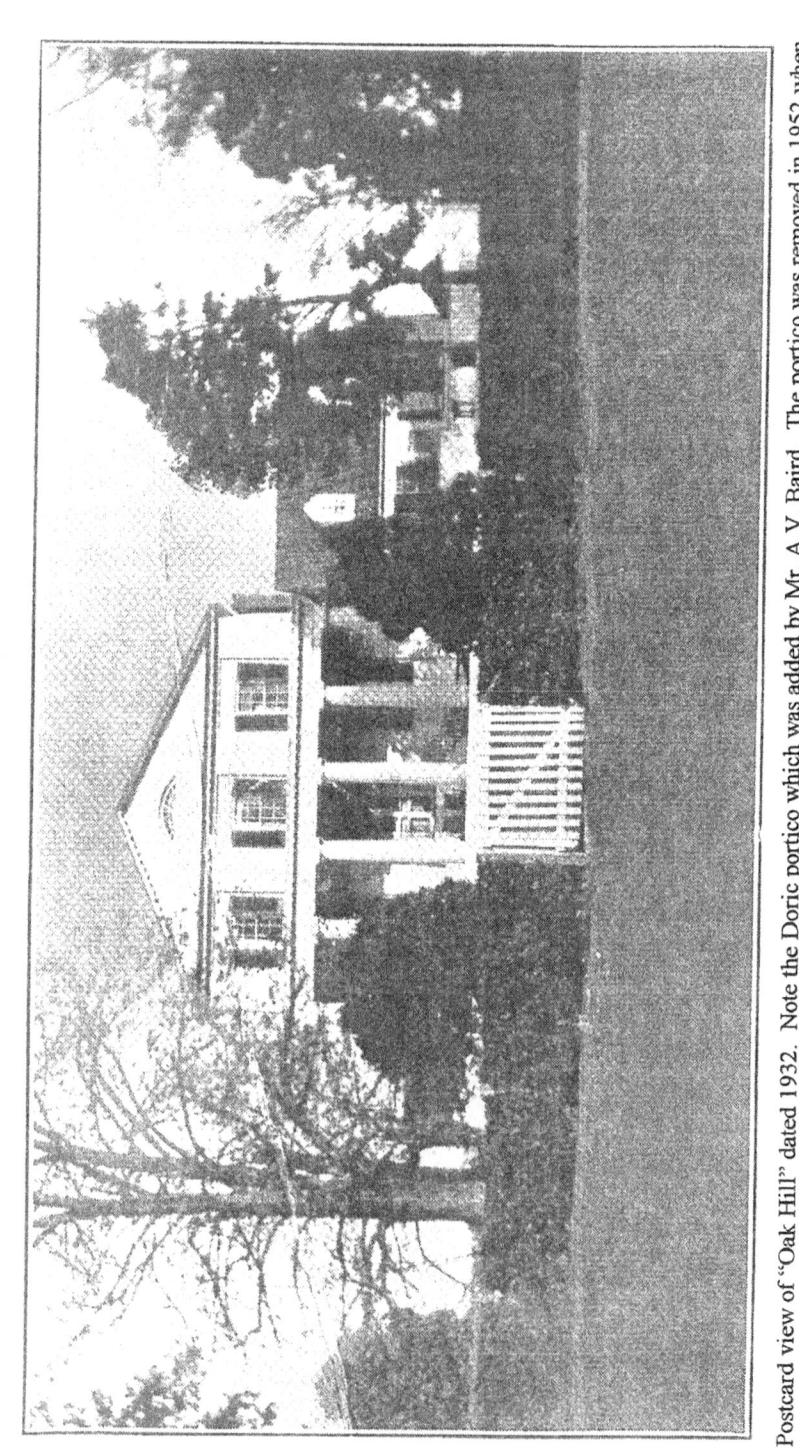

Postcard view of "Oak Hill" dated 1932. Note the Doric portico which was added by Mr. A. V. Baird. The portico was removed in 1952 when it was determined that the house originally had no front porch.

INTERIOR PICTURES OF "OAK HILL". This series of five pictures was taken by a professional photographer about 1900. They depict the rooms at "Oak Hill" as lived in by the Maddux family. They characterize the Victorians' love of clutter. Here is the stairway in the front hall of the "new" (1818) house. [From photo taken ca.1900]

Dining room at "Oak Hill," ca.1900

Bedroom at "Oak Hill," ca.1900

Bedroom at "Oak Hill," ca.1900

COBBLER MOUNTAIN HUNT HOUNDS. A meet at "Oak Hill" in the early 1930's. The hunt was formed in August 1929, under the joint mastership of S.W. McCarty and Alvin V. Baird, Sr. In 1931-32, Mr. Baird became the sole master, resigning in the spring of that year in favor of Maj. George S. Patton.

CHAPTER THREE

When the Sixth Congress convened in Philadelphia John Marshall, Representative from Virginia was there with his wife. He attended all the functions but she, obviously pregnant, was restricted in her activities. Certainly the high-fashion of the Empire period did not become her. She stayed for the most part in their rented rooms until 13 February 1800 when James Keith Marshall was born. After that she began to enjoy life in the then capital. Suddenly, near the close of the session, President John Adams named John Marshall Secretary of War. Marshall had already started for Richmond. He did not respond immediately, weighing the delights of home against the excitement of Philadelphia.

Then he was further surprised and perplexed to learn that Adams had fired his Secretary of State and named John Marshall to that office as well. He genuinely felt himself qualified for that office and decided to accept the appointment. The dilemma was alleviated in part in July by the government's decision to move to Washington, on the banks of the Potomac. Polly could not accompany him, of course; (there was no place for her to live) but it was nearer Richmond and only sixty miles from his country Seat, "Oak Hill".

The Reverend Denny Martin Fairfax died in England, 3 April 1800. He left Leeds Manor to his younger brother, Major General Philip Martin. This delayed final settlement of the Marshall purchase. On 18 October 1806 Lieutenant General Philip Martin of Leeds Castle, County

Kent deeded to Rawleigh Colston, John Marshall and James Markham Marshall the 160,382-acre Leeds Manor, acknowledging payment of £14,000 sterling or about 1s 9d per acre. In the subsequent division Rawleigh Colston claimed his third in the north part of the Manor, James Markham Marshall in the middle third, (around Markham), and John Marshall in the south.

    Suddenly, 20 January 1801, in the midst of a heated campaign for residency, President Adams appointed John Marshall to the seat of Chief Justice of the United States. Jefferson was angry at the appointment, as he expected to confer the honor on one of his own party. The presidential election was thrown into the House of Representatives where, 17 February 1801, it was decided in favor of Thomas Jefferson. Marshall had to hurry to Washington by March 4th to administer the oath. For both Jefferson and Marshall it was a bitter cup to drain.

    Polly remained in Richmond as the Chief Justice carried out the onerous duty of judicial circuit then required of members of the Supreme Court. He was sometimes in Richmond, occasionally at "Oak Hill", but generally somewhere in between or in the uncomfortable Washington boarding house, which he shared with the other Justices. In the summer of 1803 the oldest of the Marshall sons was graduated from Princeton. The Chief Justice took his family to "Oak Hill", which had come to him after his father's death. While there he attempted to buy up as much as possible of the part of the Turner grant sold to Massey.

Eventually he acquired most of it, including what would become "Ivanhoe", "The Grove", "Woodside", and "Ashleigh". An exception was "Waverley" in the northwest corner. Thomas Massey, refusing Marshall's offer, sold it to Turner Adams in 1803.

John Marshall was not in Richmond when his tenth and last child (sixth to survive), Edward Carrington Marshall, was born. On the fourth of March he administered the oath of office to his cousin Thomas Jefferson for the second time. Two days later he was on his way to Richmond to attend his son's baptism. He was, at the time, hard at work on his biography of George Washington. Thomas Marshall was beginning a law practice and writing a thesis for a master's degree from Princeton. Jaquelin was getting ready to enter Harvard College, where, during the summer the Chief Justice was to receive the honorary degree of Doctor of Laws.

The Marshall family spent the summer of 1805 at "Oak Hill" and at the Virginia springs. In September Marshall left Polly at "Oak Hill" with Mary, aged ten, James, five and the baby Edward, and returned to Richmond to take care of such of his law practice as Thomas could not handle. It was about this time that he and his son sat for the French portrait artist Charles Balthazar Julien Fevret de Saint-Mémin. Saint-Mémin had a painting gimmick that was advertised to make portraiture cheap and not take much of the sitter's time. It was called a physiognotrace, which produced a profile drawing. Saint-Mémin filled this in with only charcoal and chalk in light and deft strokes to produce a likeness. They were beautiful but his technique was such that most of them, particularly of men under thirty-five, looked very much alike. That of Thomas Marshall is incredibly handsome, but so were most of them. Marshall descendants feel that he resembled his mother, of whom only one portrait (in the Saint-Mémin style) is known to exist. It is from a drawing made by Thomas Marshall about this time. If he resembled her, so did dozens of others. They give the pleasant but entirely erroneous impression that Americans of the Federal era were as gracefully neoclassic a la Francais as Jefferson's own Virginia Capitol. John Marshall's likeness is somewhat better. It does give some sense of a brilliant mind behind the deep-set eyes, of resolute determination above the firm jaw.

In the spring of 1807 Richmond was becoming increasingly noisy and crowded by visitors and participants in the oncoming trial of Aaron Burr, former Vice-President, for treason. Early in the hot, dry summer John Marshall packed Polly and the children off to "Oak Hill". Thomas Marshall stayed in Richmond for experience in law, or militia or, possibly, just to be near his father during the long ordeal. It ended on the 20th of October and Marshall "galloped off to the Blue Ridge." Polly thought he looked older, tired.

The early part of 1809 was marred by Polly's increasing illness. John was in Washington to administer the oath of office to his friend, President James Madison. Polly was not with him but she recovered enough to attend the wedding of their son Thomas to Margaret Wardrop Lewis, daughter of Fielding and Agnes (Harwood) Lewis, 19 October 1809, at her father's James River plantation "Weyanoke". Historians have it that the Marshalls gave their son "Oak Hill" as a wedding present. If so, however, this deed does not appear to have been recorded in Fauquier County. In his will John Marshall writes, "I have given to my son Thomas the estate called Oak Hill with all my adjoining lands eastward of a line drawn along the top of the little Cobler and extending northwards to the outside Manor line, and southward to the high point to the little or north Cobler." [1]

The young couple apparently returned to Richmond, as Thomas attended the theatre on the night of 26 December 1811, only to witness the disastrous fire in which a third of the audience were killed. Margaret remained at home with their son, John, who was born at "Weyanoke" 7 May 1811. Soon after his marriage Thomas Marshall's "health failed." Historians give no clue as to the nature of his malady. It is even hinted that he suffered an affliction common to the sons of brilliant fathers who cannot hope to emulate them, a profound aversion to work. Life at "Oak Hill" was easy, although Thomas found the house in disrepair and the land much depleted. He was a good farmer and set things to rights quickly.

Fresh from the horrors of the theatre fire, the Chief Justice was not in Washington when the Supreme Court met in February of 1812. On his way there the last of January, over bad roads, the public stage overturned with a sudden jerk and his collarbone was broken. Three weeks later he was in Philadelphia but he did not stay long. He was returning from his farm outside Richmond on the Chickahominy River, 1 June 1812, when news reached him that President Madison had declared war on Great Britain.

Marshall opposed this act, which he thought unwise and unjustified, while England was grappling with the arms of Napoleon. However, be that as it may, there was work to do. Marshall was chosen to head an expedition to discover an available route to connect Virginia with the valleys of the Ohio and Mississippi. Leaving Polly and the children at "Oak Hill." with Margaret, he was soon on his way. Meanwhile Thomas Marshall, an officer in the Virginia militia was busy canvassing the Commonwealth for recruits. It was a thankless task largely unsuccessful.

Marshall brought his family back to Richmond in the autumn of 1812. Thomas was also in Richmond much of the time on recruiting business. John Marshall went to Washington in March of 1813 to administer the oath for the second time to President James Madison. There was a false sense of security in Richmond but in June the British slipped around naval vessels at Norfolk and took the town of Hampton. Polly left for "Oak Hill" with Mary, John, James and Edward. Thomas and Jaquelin remained in Richmond with the militia.

At "Oak Hill", 18 September 1813, seventeen year old Mary Marshall married her first cousin, Jaquelin Burwell Harvie.
On the 5th of November Margaret (Lewis) Marshall gave birth to her second child, Agnes Harwood Marshall.

Polly and the children remained at "Oak Hill" during the anxious winter when the British were threatening. In August of 1814 refugees from Washington told her of the sack of the city. Colonel James Monroe, at the head of the militia had gone out to meet them with a small force of whom Thomas Marshall was one. However, the emergency soon passed and "Mr. Madison's War" was over. Polly and the children were in Richmond before Christmas.

At "Oak Hill" Margaret Marshall gave birth to their third child, Mary, 25 March 1816. It was about this time that Thomas Marshall and his wife decided that they needed a new house. The old one was in fine shape but lacked the amenities they felt they needed. In the eighteenth century manner the rooms were small and could not easily be thrown together for entertaining. What was needed was a Federal style house with large rooms that could be combined, wide halls and a grand staircase. The temple-form plan found in most pattern books of the period exactly fitted their needs. It was a two-storey house with a pedimented front wall in the classic manner, with halls across the front at both levels and two large parlours behind, connected by wide folding doors.

It has been stated by many biographers that the Chief Justice provided homes for his children on his estates in Fauquier County. That appears to be untrue, at least in the case of "Oak Hill". He gave them the land. After that they could shift for themselves, or nearly so. A letter written by Thomas Marshall to a builder, John Armstrong, near Jeffersonton, Culpeper County seems to prove that point [2] Dated 16 July 1817, it reads:

"Mr. John Armstrong
Sir: The excessive and unexpected depression in the price of produce and other property since this time last year has made it necessary for me to change my plans of operation on the subject of building. I find it impossible for me at present, or perhaps for some time to come, with such a house as I had in contemplation last year, and which I then had every reason to think I could build with ease. It is my intention at present to make an addition of brick, with two rooms and a passage on each floor, to the north end of the house in which I now reside. This addition I propose to erect next year unless the commissioners for laying off a turnpike road from Manassas Gap to Middleburg should unfortunately think fit to lay off the road in such a manner as for it to pass just by my house. There is some reason to fear this may be the case, but the

probabilities are against it. Whatever course it is to take will be determined in a few weeks. In the
meantime I should like to see you at the next Fauquier Court, where I expect to be without [fail?] and where I can have the opportunity of speaking to you more fully on the subject. It is my wish to retain you for the work, and hope we shall be able to make a satisfactory agreement. Saunders[3] has made nearly 100,000 bricks and will complete the balance this season. Almost all the necessary plank is prepared, and I now consider it fortunate that the scantling was not got ready by the man whom I engaged for the purpose.

       I remain yours &c.
       Thomas Marshall.

  The house described by Marshall is the one he built the following year although he apparently expected to lower its cost by attaching it directly to the old building. Fortunately Armstrong, or someone, talked him out of that, as the present house stands with its east wall in line with the west wall of the old house, and removed from it about eleven feet. Originally, the two houses were not connected in any way.
  The proposed turnpike was apparently to connect Middleburg with a point in the old Dumfries Road near

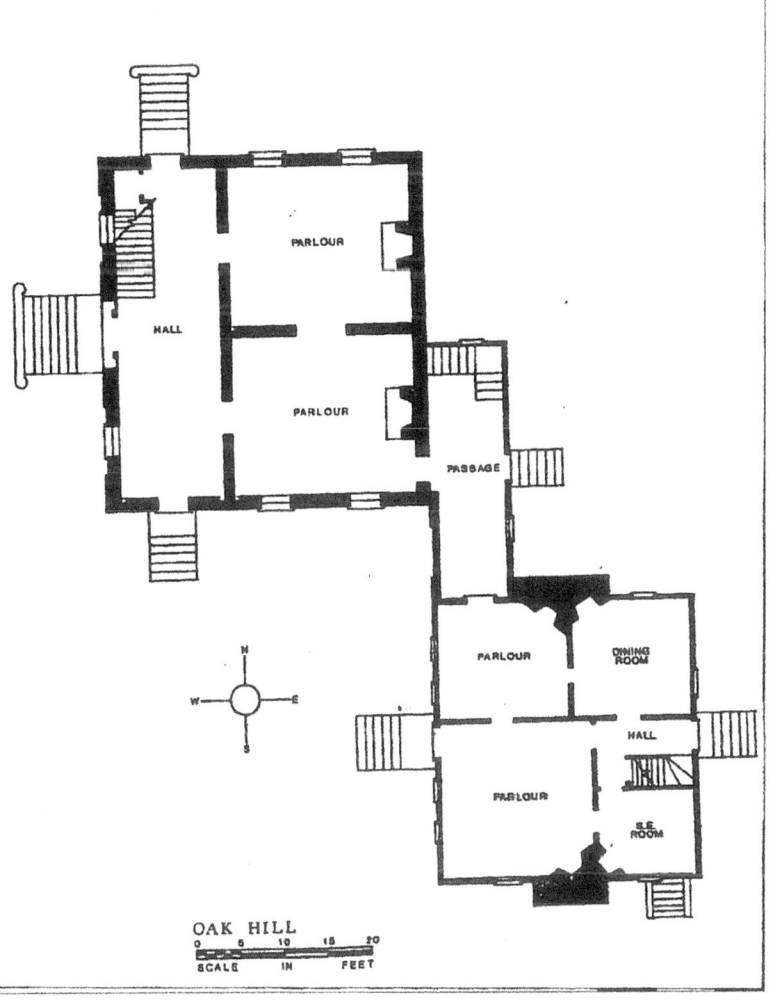

Emmanuel Church. It would have to swing needlessly far south to pass close to "Oak Hill", but Marshall was taking no chances. The turnpike was never built but part of it may be reflected in Route 713 from Emmanuel Church to "Flint Hill" on Long Branch of Goose Creek.

The financial situation apparently eased in 1818 and the house was finished in early 1819 in time for the birth of the Marshall's fourth child, Fielding Lewis Marshall, born 29 March 1819.

Somewhat surprisingly the finish, both inside and out, of the new house is inferior to that of the house built in 1773. On the outside the brick is lightly stuccoed, as was the fashion, with wide, slightly projecting, pilasters on the west front. The whole is crowned by a modified Doric cornice with mutules and guttae. The pilasters appear to support a pediment in which is a. shallow lunette. The entrance treatment has double, three panel, doors flanked by sidelights and paneled pilasters, over which is a blank fluted fan. All are set in an opening under an elliptical arch. On the sides, at the ends of-the stair hall, are doors set in shallow recesses with blank lunettes.

From a watercolor, undated but obviously painted before the Civil War when the house was in its original state, we know that the entrance was approached directly by a simple, wide, flight of steps. Otherwise the exterior today looks very much as it did in 1819 when viewed from the west. The window sash is double hung, six-over-six instead of nine-over-nine as in the old house.

The chimneys are inside and both on the former east wall, which was otherwise blank. This peculiar arrangement was intended to conceal the chimneys and thus not to spoil the temple-form profile. It is probable that the shutters are original with the house, as they came into use late in the eighteenth century and fit neatly between the pilasters of the west front.

Within, the finish is of good quality, but rather run-of-the-mill for the period. The walls are plastered and each main room has a simple molded cornice. Doors have symmetrically molded trim and corner blocks with rosettes. The two-flight rectangular stair at the north end of the entrance hall has an open string with brackets at the ends. Mantels have wide shelves over friezes with diagonal reeding and center panels decorated with elliptical ornaments and flanked by attenuated columns. They are good without being exceptional. As none of the Marshall furniture remains within the house, we must assume that it was typical of the Federal period, massive in scale but simple in design.

Although Chief Justice John Marshall visited the new house at "Oak Hill" often, as he did the homes of his other children nearby, Polly came "up country" less and less frequently. She was almost a recluse in her room in the house in Richmond, having assumed, at the age of fifty-one, the privileges of an old lady.

Her husband, at sixty-two, was full of life as ever. An acquaintance found the Chief Justice occupying his cottage at Fauquier White Sulphur Springs in the summer of 1823. Polly was not with him. The cottage adjoined that of his friend James Monroe and they often met there to take the waters together.

At "Oak Hill" in the years between 1819 and 1829 life followed its normal course. Thomas Marshall had represented Fauquier County in the Virginia Assembly in 1814 and 1819 but his anti-slavery views cost him his seat in 1823. However by 1827 the anti-slavery faction under his leadership was strong enough to return him to the House of Delegates.

Three more children were born at "Oak Hill": Anne Lewis Marshall, 2 August 1823; Margaret Lewis Marshall, born 29 October 1823 (according to Paxton) and Thomas Marshall, Jr., born 17 January 1826. Although the birth dates of Anne and Margaret are impossible as given, it may be assumed that Margaret was born a year later.

In the summer of 1824 Polly paid her last visit to "Oak Hill". Traveling over the rough roads "shook her frame." She found the place a center of county politics. The children made her nervous, the swarm of guests tired her. Her husband brought her home earlier than usual. In Richmond there was a new distraction, the uproar over the visit to Virginia of General the Marquis de Lafayette. It was during Lafayette's visit, 23 August 1825, at Warrenton that Chief Justice John Marshall delivered his celebrated toast to Fauquier County: [4]

"I can never forget that this county was the residence of the revered author of my being, who continued to be your representative, until his military character first, and his removal afterwards, rendered him ineligible; that in this county I first breathed the vital air; that in it my infancy was cradled and my youth reared up and encouraged; that in the first dawn of manhood I marched from it with the gallant young men of the day to that glorious conflict which gave independence to these states, and birth to this mighty nation; that immediately on my return, I was chosen unanimously to represent them in the legislature, and that they did not cease to support me till I ceased to reside among them .. Here my affections as well as my interest still remain, and all my sons are planted among you. With so many motives for receiving the kindness of today with peculiar gratitude, allow me, gentlemen, to indulge the feeling it excites."

Here he raised his glass to toast:

"The people of Fauquier.. Brave soldiers in time of war, good citizens in time of peace and intelligent patriots at all times.'"

Thomas Marshall seemed to be prospering at "Oak Hill". He was an innovative farmer and was now experimenting with a large roller intended to compact the soil after a corn crop so that wheat could be planted. However, in February 1826 he wrote his mother asking to borrow $200. His father furnished the money, but cautioned his wife against such indulgence. He did not encourage his children to go into debt. The Chief Justice visited his sons' plantations and found them lush and green in the late summer of 1828. He no longer rode horseback, but on a stick gig which was kinder to his rear. From "Oak Hill" he purchased one of the fine horses Thomas was breeding there, for delivery in the fall. In September Thomas wrote his father that the roller was working splendidly, but that he had been so busy seeding that he had quite forgotten to send the horse.

It appears that there was nothing to prepare Thomas Marshall for the blow that fell on his house early in 1829. Margaret (Lewis) Marshall died suddenly, in childbirth 2 February 1829. She was only thirty-seven, and she left behind seven children ranging in age from eighteen to three years old. Thomas expressed the deepest grief to his father, who wrote his wife with mild surprise, "It [the letter] is serious and very religious." Perhaps he had not noticed such traits in his son before. Later the Chief Justice wrote, "He says that he is very much occupied with his children and I hope that will gradually restore him to happiness. He retains John with him and superintends his education."

At eighteen Thomas Marshall had been at Princeton. John Marshall, his son, did attend the University of Virginia later, as did his brothers Fielding Lewis and Thomas Marshall, Jr. Their father was returned to the Virginia House of Delegates in 1830 and continued there until his death.

Mary Willis (Ambler) Marshall, "Polly", died in Richmond on Christmas Day 1831. The Chief Justice had not been well in October and had gone to Philadelphia where he had an operation for kidney stones by a doctor with the unlikely name of Philip Syng Physick. Returning to Richmond 19 November, he soon realized that his wife was dying. The Chief Justice was inconsolable, but he was present at the spring session of the Supreme Court in February. He continued living in the Richmond house when not in Washington, accompanied by his son Thomas when the legislature was in session.

In 1833 the Chief Justice was seventy-eight and still sitting on the Supreme Court, but it was obvious that his health was failing and that he must think about retirement. He had no desire to remain in Richmond, and sought a home with his sons in Fauquier County. "Oak Hill" was out of the question because of the absence of its mistress. His fourth son, James Keith Marshall, had married, 22 December 1821, Claudia Hamilton Burwell, daughter of Nathaniel and Ann (Willis) Burwell of "White Hall." On land from the Fairfax purchase, given him by his father, young Keith Marshall built "Leeds", a substantial house within easy riding distance of his brothers. Plans were made in 1833 to build an addition to the house at a cost of $900. John Marshall sent his son the money, $500 in September and $400 the following spring. In October the foundation was dug, but the old man was never to occupy it.

Early in 1835 the Chief Justice participated in the decisions of the Supreme Court but he was visibly ill. In June he collapsed on his way to visit his wife's grave in Richmond's Shocktoe Hill Cemetery. He was taken as quickly as possible to Philadelphia where he came again under the care of Dr. Physick. His liver was found greatly enlarged and there were other signs of malignancy. His son, Edward Carrington Marshall, was with him and, when his stay became longer than expected, Thomas Marshall rushed to replace him. On June 29th, passing through Baltimore, Thomas Marshall sought shelter from a sudden thundershower in the scaffolding surrounding the old courthouse (on the site of the present courthouse). There bricks, dislodged from a crumbling chimney, struck him and fractured his skull. He died soon after, but the Chief Justice was not informed of his death.

Chief Justice John Marshall himself died 6 July 1835 in his eightieth year. He left a long and carefully considered will in which Thomas Marshall's ownership of "Oak Hill" was fully confirmed. [5] Thomas Marshall died intestate at the age of fifty-one.

At the time of Thomas Marshall's death the "Oak Hill" estate contained upwards of three thousand acres. [6] It comprised (1) the entire Turner grant of 1,700 acres, less about 250 acres belonging to "Waverly", then belonging to Susan Q. (Elliott) Curlette, wife of Dr. Curlette; (2) a long strip of densely wooded land out of the Fairfax land, containing 714 acres, and (3) the Harrison purchase and several other minor tracts southwest of "Oak Hill". To divide this equally among the seven heirs of Thomas Marshall was no easy task.

John Marshall, the eldest son, of course, inherited the "mansion house", but presumably because of the value of the house and outbuildings, to make things equal, he was given one hundred fewer acres than his siblings. He was thirty-three when his father died and married 20 November 1837 Anne Eliza Blackwell, daughter of William and Anne Sparke (Gordon) Blackwell of Fauquier.

Agnes Harwood Marshall married 4 May 1836 General Alexander Galt Taliaferro. She shared with her sister, Mary, 279 acres south and west of the mansion. Mary Marshall married, January 1837, William Archer, a Richmond lawyer.

Fielding Lewis Marshall inherited 313 acres west of "Oak Hill", on which he built "Ivanhoe". He married 10 April 1843, Rebecca F. Coke.

Anne Lewis Marshall was given 313 acres north of the manor house, on which "Woodside" was built. She married, 2 January 1845, James-Fitzgerald Jones.

Margaret Lewis Marshall was given 313 acres west of her sister Anne.

She married 25 September 1845 John Thomas Smith, her cousin. They built "Ashleigh" from plans apparently obtained from the Natchez, Mississippi, area where there are similar houses.

Thomas Marshall, Jr., was given 815 acres in the southwest corner. Of the Turner grant as well as the so-called Harrison purchase south of it. The reason for the enormous inequality is that the Harrison purchase and adjoining land was under lease. It was up to Thomas, Jr., to collect rents and distribute the proceeds among the other heirs.

To all the foregoing tracts except the last was attached an average of 135 acres of the timberland in Leeds Manor along the west border. Thomas Marshall's tract, because of its position, had sufficient timber to meet his needs. He married, 24 August 1848, Annie Maria Barton, daughter of David Walker Barton, a distinguished Winchester attorney, under whom Thomas had studied law after his graduation from the University of Virginia.

There were two mills on the "Oak Hill" estate. One of them, on the line between "Oak Hill" and "Woodside", was apparently sold by the Chief Justice in 1804 to Robert Henniford.[7] The other, farther up the run and nearly opposite the manor house, apparently, fell to Fielding Lewis Marshall who rebuilt the mill house in 1844. He apparently sold it to Thomas Turner Adams.

Thus "Oak Hill", the manor house of over 3,000 acres, was reduced to only 213 acres, plus an additional 135 acres of timber land nearly a mile away. The 3,000 acres had barely supported the life style of the Marshalls in Thomas's day. His son John could hardly be expected to do as well on 367, even by leasing his sisters' land to the south. The division of Thomas Marshall's estate was not completed until after 1842 and before 1845. John Marshall took over the management of his inheritance after his marriage in 1837. He was then twenty-six.

John Marshall was unwilling, possibly unable, to give up the life style to which he was accustomed. Paxton writes,

"Here he lived a life of a scholar and literary gentleman, and by his profuse hospitality made Oak Hill a home of delights. But he was unable to keep up this free and liberal life, and in 1852, sold the estate to his younger brother Thomas." [8]

One feels sorry for John, struggling mightily with an impossible task, scholarly no doubt, but without his father's talent for farming. He moved to Culpeper County where his wife died two years later; he suddenly, presumably of a heart attack, followed her in less than a month.

Thomas Marshall, Jr., twenty-six in 1852, had done considerably better since his father had died. He settled at "Shady Oak", near Winchester, which he farmed successfully. He moved to "Oak Hill" in 1853 and lived there until his wife's death in 1861. They had five children. He was with his wife when she died in child-birth 11 February 1861.

On the night of 16 October 1859 Marshall had galloped post-haste to Harpers Ferry and had become a voluntary aide to General Thomas Jonathan Jackson with the rank of captain. After his wife's death the children were dispatched to Winchester under the care of their maternal grandmother. Captain Thomas Marshall saw long and hard service during the war, ending in November of 1864 as colonel in command of the 7th Virginia Cavalry, C. S. A. ("The Laurel Brigade") In an engagement near Winchester, 12 November 1864, Colonel Thomas Marshall was shot through the heart.

"Oak Hill" was apparently unoccupied during the War except for a few domestics. While the house and immediate outbuildings suffered no material damage, outlying barns and other structures, fences and timber were largely destroyed. Livestock was taken and the land did not benefit from four years of neglect.

Colonel Thomas Marshall did not leave a will but he did leave a memorandum, written at Staunton, Virginia, 7 October 1864:[9]

"In view of the uncertainty of my life I desire to indicate in a general way the condition of my property, & my wishes with respect to its management.

In consequence of my brother F. Lewis Marshall being already burdened with the management of an involved estate of my elder brother, I desire my brother-in-law W. Strother Barton to take charge of my estate, in the event of my decease, and by consultation with Mr. Philip Williams (Winchester) & my brother F. Lewis Marshall, proceed to take such course in the settlement of it as he may deem best."

He then lists such outstanding debts as he can recall totaling $18,325. He lists assets, including "Oak Hill", then about 650 acres, a mountain farm of about 450 acres in the Free State, a few servants, a small amount of livestock, some household furniture, and two bonds amounting to $850 which he had turned over to his father-in-law, D. W. Barton, recently deceased, for the use of his children. There was also due a balance from Mountjoy, "who lives between Oak Hill and Salem", for land he and his brother had sold.[10] There were two Confederate bonds in the hands of John W. Kincheloe, commissary of the 7th Regiment, and one for $900 in the hands of his sister, Anne Lewis (Marshall) Jones.

William Strother Barton, brother of Maria (Barton) Marshall, was a distinguished Winchester lawyer well qualified to be executor of the estate and care for his five nieces and nephews, (two of whom apparently did not reach maturity). All too quickly, however, it was realized that Colonel Marshall's recollection of the amount of his debts was far from complete. He had given many small notes and had borrowed substantially from his brother and sisters. Furthermore, after the War, many of his assets were worthless, including his "few servants" and his Confederate bonds. Not surprisingly Barton was soon faced by a suit in chancery, styled "Marshall, Trustee, &c vs. Marshall's Administrator." [11]

When all was said and done it was found that the indebtedness of the Marshall estate was about double the amount Colonel Marshall had estimated, namely, $36,139.80. It was not possible to even begin its settlement until "Oak Hill" was sold. The Court so ordered by decree dated 7 September 1866. The advertisement for the public sale of "Oak Hill" farm reads as follows: [12]

PUBLIC SALE OF THE "OAK HILL" FARM

Marshall Trustee, &c.]
vs] IN CHANCERY
Marshall's Administrator]

Pursuant to a decree in this case granted by the County Court of Fauquier County, Va., appointing me Special Commissioner to make sale of a certain portion of the real estate of the late Thos. Marshall, dec, d, I will on Wednesday, August 1st, 1866 on the premises, offer at public sale, the entire tract of land known as "Oak Hill" Farm.

This tract contains 650 ACRES OF LAND divided in proper proportions into Meadow, Upland, and Timber Land, and is watered by flowing streams and never-failing Springs, making it rank among the best of Fauquier grain and pasture lands. The improvements consist of a fine large DWELLIING HOUSE and all necessary outbuildings; a large Barn somewhat out of repair and a goodstone blacksmith's shop, a good mill site and the lower walls of a mill most of the fencing destroyed during the war has been restored &c.................Possession given January 1st 1867.

W. S. Barton, special Comm'r.

Apparently the mill had fallen victim to the War but the rest could be made usable with a little tender loving care. John Shumate, a local farmer, was renting the place and was prepared to show prospective purchasers its many charms including the sweeping panorama of the Blue Ridge as seen from its west doorway. The sale was held as advertised with William Knight of Cecil County, Maryland as the highest bidder. He offered $54.25 per acre, or a total of $29,404.05, spread in equal payments over four years.[13] Interestingly the value of the mansion house itself was not considered in the deal. Knight was not seeking a home, merely speculating in land. So passed from the Marshall family "Oak Hill" which had been their home for more than one hundred years. The home was gone, but the chancery suit lingered on. William Strother Barton died 28 July 1868, worn out, possibly, by the claims and counter claims in the chancery suit and his inability to satisfy any of the participants. The Court appointed his brother and law partner, Robert T. Barton, as Special Commissioner 9 April 1869. In a long deposition, dated 1 February 1871, R. T. Barton, who had been in the fray from the beginning, recited the long history of his brother's stewardship. The chancery suit was continued until 1888. All of the original participants were long since dead, including Robert T. Barton. Robert Taylor Scott was then Commissioner. On the 7th of September 1888 the Circuit Court of Fauquier County decreed that all funds had been disbursed and the case was closed.[14] No one was satisfied but, as with most chancery suits, no one was greatly surprised.

CHAPTER FOUR

Whatever had been the interest that caused William Knight to buy "Oak Hill" in 1867, it did not last long. He may have visited it and possibly farmed it for a while with an overseer, but he certainly never lived there. By 1873 he was prepared to take a substantial loss on his investment. He sold it 4 April 1873 to Charles M. Kefauver.[1] Kefauver held the property a little more than three years. Taking a further loss, he sold it 15 December 1876 to Franklin Webster Maddux [2] for $20,000.

Franklin Webster Maddux, usually known as F. Webb Maddux, was a successful merchant/farmer in the town of Marshall. However, he liked to say that "Oak Hill", which he had long coveted, was bought with the proceeds of cockfighting and breeding fighting cocks. His cocks were famous far and wide, and one even had the distinction of posing for his portrait. It is said that, on one occasion, he rode the train to New Orleans with a cock under his arm beneath his coat. That story is declared apocryphal by his descendants, but he did accompany his champions on many long journeys and was prepared to bet on their prowess when he reached his destination.

He soon made "Oak Hill" habitable once more and made certain additions in the fashion of the eighteen eighties that seem somewhat incongruous. In the first place he built a Victorian veranda on the west front and on both sides of the 1818 house. Although the veranda lacked the gimcrackery so dear to the Victorian taste, it did darken the first floor rooms and some how trivialized the architectural design. He also, for reasons quite obscure today, closed and weather boarded over the central doorway on the west front of the 1773 house. This would be difficult to believe if there were not, contemporary photographs to prove it, in which the shadow of the old opening appears. Additionally he had constructed a shed-roofed porch over the steps to the east (originally entrance) door of the 1773 house. This crude bit of construction rests on log foundations.

We are fortunate in having photographs of the interior of 'Oak Hill' made about 1900 during the Maddux ownership.[3] The wall and ceilings are covered with wallpaper in bold repetitive pattern and bright color. Across them in profusion pictures are strewn, some of them, we are told, watercolors by Maddux's accomplished daughter, Emma. Little, if any, of the Marshall furniture remains, although some of it dates from the first half of the nineteenth century. It is heavy, ornate and there is too much of it. Every surface having room to decorate is decorated and piled high with bric-a-brac. The whole effect is cluttered and, in its Victorian way, charming. There is one piece of furniture, which Maddux said that he had bought, from a sale at "Waveland", the home of Colonel John Augustine Washington, and that it had once been at "Mount Vernon". This simple Sheraton-style, banquet dining room table, is visible in the photograph of the dining room and appears very like some tables at "Mount Vernon" today.

It is known that the table in the family dining room at "Mount Vernon" was not there in Washington's day. Possibly this one was.

Colonel F. Webb Maddux entertained a party of his friends at "Oak Hill" during Christmas week of 1903. One of them wrote about it the following September.[4] The account is signed "B", probably Colonel Edmund Berkeley, who was one of the guests. The splendid house with chimneys built of bricks "brought from England" [sic], commanding a view from the front portico "truly grand and unsurpassed by any I have ever seen." The lavish hospitality is described in some detail. Colonel Maddux's distinction in being the most celebrated raiser of game fowls in the United States, "if not in the world" is touched upon. "The Colonel realizes from his fowls alone about fifteen hundred dollars per annum."

Colonel Berkeley notes that their joy was not lessened by the knowledge General Lafayette and other celebrities had once been seated around the same dining table. He mentioned that he was probably the only living person who had been held in Lafayette's arms and been kissed by him. He takes considerable umbrage when one of his friends remarks that Lafayette would be unlikely to do the same that day! Since Chief Justice John Marshall was a visitor at "Mount Vernon" during the General Washington's lifetime it is probable that he, too, had dined at the same table.

Berkeley notes that the furnishings of the mansion were elegant, but mentions only one specific item.

MADDUX FAMILY AT "OAK HILL". F. Webster Maddux, Sr. had the Victorian porch erected on the "new house." The "old house" had become the kitchen and servants' quarters. The Maddux family with guests and servants are pictured in this early photograph.

Parlour at "Oak Hill" during the ownership of the Maddux family.

MADDUX FAMILY AT "OAK HILL," gathered on side porch, ca.1900. (on lower step) Emma Belle; (on back row) Owen Thompson, George R. Thompson, Alice L. Maddux, F. Webb Maddux, Sr. (holding G. Richard Thompson, Jr.); (middle row) Billie Brent, Kittie Maddux, Emma (Maddux) Thompson, T. Henderson Maddux; (front row) Maddux Thompson, Nannie Fischer, Tom Fischer.

FRANKLIN WEBSTER MADDUX, SR. (1838-1905). Owner of "Oak Hill," from 1876 until his death in 1905. This picture dates from about the time of his purchase of the farm.

FRANKLIN WEBSTER MADDUX, SR. (1838-1905). Son of Thomas Lawrence Maddux of "Westwood," Confederate veteran, farmer, cattleman and merchant of Fauquier Co. He was noted for his hospitality and had the Victorian porch added to "Oak Hill" where he entertained his many guests.

Thomas Henderson Maddux and Franklin Webster Maddux, sons of F. Webb Maddux, Sr., and heirs to "Oak Hill," upon their father's death in 1905.

ALVIN VORIS BAIRD, SR. A native of Akron, Ohio, Mr. Baird graduated from Harvard (1904) and the law school of Harvard University. In 1914, seven years after receiving his law degree, he purchased "Oak Hill" from the Maddux brothers and moved to Virginia. He restored his beloved "Oak Hill," was engaged in raising cattle, and active in his church, polo and fox hunting. He was one of the founders and MFH of the Cobbler Mountain Hunt in 1929. He died at "Oak Hill" in June 1964, just a few months after the death of his wife, Rawson Kay Baird.

WHERE MARSHALL LIVED

Home of the Celebrated Chief Justice of the United States.

A Picturesque Virginia Place, Which is Still Preserved, Although Not Owned by the Descendants.

Special Correspondence of The Evening Star.
WARRENTON, Va., September 10, 1896. Starting at this point, a fine summer drive of about fifteen miles through a country that once bristled with bayonets and echoed with the artillery of hostile armies, but which today is marked by peace and good husbandry, leads up to one of the most beautiful pastoral regions of Virginia. It was there, near the town which bears his name, that Chief Justice Marshall had his home.

The house is a good type of colonial architecture, constructed, as it is, on the simple and commodious lines of that period, with a veranda on all sides leading into a hallway which extends lengthwise and opens into a spacious drawing room and dining salon, with big cheerful windows and high-pitched ceilings.

A wide stairway winds up to the second story, which consists of three bed chambers. The original structure, which was added to by Thomas Marshall, the son of the chief justice, is finished in carved cherry. A frieze encircles one of the rooms which is embellished with quaint designs that were cut with a penknife. There is an entire absence of nails throughout the house, the flooring betrays primitive methods of carpentry, and the walls, the logs of which were imported from Europe and hauled across country from Fredericksburg, are stuccoed with mortar, which is such a common feature in the rural architecture of those days.

The place takes its name from a superb grove of oaks which cluster about the house with almost human affection. The views of the Blue Ridge from every point are magnificent, bringing under the eye a bold and rugged stretch of foothills, with the mountains a few miles beyond, undulating like so many blue billows.

The present owner of "Oakville" is Mr. Walsh Maddux, who is a large landowner and one of the substantial men of Fauquier county, contiguous to his residence is a farm of a thousand highly cultivated acres, which are principally in grass of the Kentucky variety.

Mr. Maddux is a picturesque figure and popular character in this section of the state. He was a good fighter during the war, and followed the plume of Mosby. He is a man of commanding presence, standing over six feet two inches, with a robust physique and massive frame.

About fifty-five years of age, he is the youngest of thirteen children, and he himself has an interesting family of three daughters and two sons.

Mr. Maddux employs negro labor, and there is an atmosphere about the place that recalls plantation life. There are types among his servants that have interested famous sketch artists, and the proprietor himself has a touch of the southern planter about his personality which betrays itself in the hospitable reception accorded to those who have visited this lovely old Virginia estate.

The parlour was dominated by a splendid stuffed specimen of the great American hawk, four feet from wingtip to wingtip, shot by one of Maddux's sons. The party, all male except the hostess and her accomplished daughters, had a lovely time.

F. Webb Maddux died in 1905. In his will dated 12 November 1902, he left "Oak Hill" jointly to his two sons, Thomas Henderson Maddux and Franklin Webster Maddux, Jr.[5] Neither wanted to live there and, obviously, if they were to realize on their inheritance, the property must be sold. They asked $52,000, or approximately $100 per acre. In early 1914 they found a purchaser in Alvin Voris Baird, son of Charles Baird of Akron, Ohio. Alvin Baird was then practicing law in New York but was searching for farming property in Virginia. One day he came upon a booklet published by the Southern Railway in which the magnificent panorama seen from the west door of "Oak Hill" was shown. He then decided that "Oak Hill" was for him. He offered $46,000, which the Maddux brothers declined.

Baird promptly withdrew the offer, on a rather flimsy excuse, feigning indifference. The Madduxes brought in a stalking horse, or, perhaps, stalking mare would be more appropriate. She was Miss Helen Morgan, a wealthy but flighty heiress from Forest Hills, Illinois, who had been renting the house and proposed to buy it upon her marriage to a certain Mr. Bailey. Baird questioned the value of the farmland and proposed calling in a nationally known agricultural engineers Joseph Wing of Mechanicsburg, Ohio, to value the land.

However, before Wing had a chance to visit the property, Baird's eagerness to obtain it prompted him to raise his offer to $48,000. The Maddux brothers, not at all certain that Mr. Wing's assessment would be in their favor, promptly accepted. Finally, 21 August 1914, after a long hot summer of negotiation, "Oak Hill" was deeded to Alvin V. Baird.[6]

In the last few weeks before closing the deal Alvin Baird had been complaining bitterly that delay in clearing the title had delayed his working on the house. He was well aware that the Victorian porch was inappropriate and must be replaced. He had already engaged a New York architect, Stanley Parker, to design an "architecturally correct" entrance portico. Parker, whatever his other qualifications, had not the faintest idea what a temple-form Federal house in the Virginia Piedmont was supposed to look like. Apparently he thought the house was Greek Revival (1835-1855), which it is not. He designed a heavy, tetrastyle Doric portico in the best Greek Revival idiom, which was promptly built. The Doric portico was not the only anacronism committed by Parker. He could see that there had been a door in the center of the west wall of the 1773 house. He reopened the door, building it in a wide frame with a pediment on top, in what he conceived to be the Colonial manner. That, too, was a mistake.

Parker also extended the main roof to the east to cover two-storey porches, and carried out some minor interior alterations to allow for baths.

These alterations were hardly completed before, in 1916, Albert J. Beveridge's "The Life of John Marshall" [7] was published. In it (Volume I, page 56) is reproduced a watercolor of "Oak Hill", painted during the period of the Marshall residency. The name of the artist is unknown. It was found among the Marshall memorabilia inherited by Thomas Marshall Smith of Baltimore. It showed unmistakably that there was not, and never had been, a porch on the west front of the 1818 house in Marshall's time. The only entrance treatment was the double door with its sidelights and carved fan above, recessed under the elegant elliptical arch.

Something else was evident but less plainly seen. The west doorway of the 1773 building was not as had been conjecturally restored. It was a six-panel door set in a narrow frame with a transom above to raise its lintel in line with the window heads. Instead of being crowded and overdone it had the simplicity of the south or garden front of "Kenmore" which has precisely the same arrangement.

In 1934 Thomas A. Franzioli Jr., then a recent graduate of the architectural school of the University of Pennsylvania, was commissioned by the Office of National Parks, Buildings and Restorations of the Department of the Interior, to make complete measured drawings of "Oak Hill." He was instructed apparently to omit all known twentieth century construction and show the house as it had been in the early nineteenth century.

Fransioli was familiar with the early watercolor, which is noted on the drawings. He therefore omitted Parker's Doric portico and the two-storey porches on the east front of the 1818 house. He indicated his doubts of the authenticity of the west door of the older house by dotting in the conjectured pediment above. He also omitted the makeshift porch over the east entrance.

Alvin Baird was naturally dismayed by these revelations as he was genuinely interested in having "Oak Hill" look as much as possible as it had in the time of Chief Justice John Marshall. When the Doric porch showed signs of needing repair in 1948, Baird decided that it was a good time to tear it down and restore the facade to its original appearance. This he did in 1952. Only one unfortunate addition remains: a leanto of uncertain date, north of the 1773 houses completely covers the lower part of the superb eighteenth century chimney.

An historical survey of old homes in Fauquier County was sponsored during this same period (The Great Depression) by the Public Works Administration. The article on "Oak Hill" adds an item of interest not found elsewhere;[9] an interview with the last Marshall born at "Oak Hill":

>"Today [1 March 1937], I [Mrs. Frances B. Foster] paid a visit to Mrs. Fanny Jones Holt, to have her give me some of her early recollections concerning Oak Hill, her birthplace,...

Mrs. Holt is the mother of Jack Holt, the movie actor, and the daughter of Colonel Thomas, grandson of Chief Justice Marshall. Fanny Marshall Holt was the last Marshall to be born at Oak Hill. Her mother died when she was six years old, and she remembers with great vividness, that occasion. How her father, Col. Marshalls sang hymns to her dying mother - "I want to be an angel", being one she especially recalls. Col. Thomas Marshall was a deeply religious man, and had planned to enter the ministry after the War. During the War between the States his old Mammy was dying, and he got leave to come to see her. Mrs. Holt says he, himself gave her last communion, and sat by her deathbed.

Mrs. Holt is now in her eighties, but is a beautiful woman and possessed of great charm and personality, ...

A rather unusual coincidence is that Mr. Holt [an Episcopal minister] was the great nephew of Chief Justice White, and Mrs. Holt, herself, great-grand-daughter of Chief Justice Marshall, had for her most intimate friend, the girl who became the wife of Chief Justice White."

Mrs. Holt also related that her father is buried in Winchester, near the graves of General Turner Ashby and his brother, Richard Ashby, who were both killed in action during the Civil War. Her mother is buried at "Oak Hill" in the family cemetery near the west end of the houses.

A vast concourse of people gathered on the sweeping lawns of "Oak Hill", 12 September 1928 to celebrate the one hundred and seventy-third anniversary of the birthday of John Marshall. Incidentally, they met to launch the proposed John Marshall Highway (Route 53) from Washington through Thoroughfare Gap then, passing by "Oak Hill", to Manassas Gap and Front Royal, where it linked with the Sky Line Drive through the Shenandoah National Park and with the Valley Pike. [10]

It was an all-day celebration with free box lunches and refreshments at the expense of the Commissioners. Everyone was there. Speeches began in the morning and continued all day. The last was given by the Honorable R. Walton Moore, Congressman from the Eighth Congressional District of Virginia. Congressman Moore was of the old school of political declamation; he did not make speeches, he delivered orations. His booming voice seemed to reach to the Blue Ridge and back in thundering echoes. He called upon the shades of the founding fathers, of Washington, Jefferson and Robert E. Lee to witness the glory of the occasion. Gesticulating widely, he refought the Civil War and, miraculously, the South won. Those who listened, spellbound, were not sure of his point but all agreed that it was a humdinger of a speech. They never forgot it!

Alvin V. Baird made a will in 1951 leaving his wife, Rawson (Kay) Baird, a life interest in his estate, after which it was to be divided equally among his three children or their heirs.[11] His wife predeceased him at "Oak Hill," 9 March 1964. He followed her in death less than three months later, 6 June 1964.

The following September "Oak Hill" was sold by the heirs, Alvin Voris Baird: Jr., Gordon P. Baird and Marie (Baird) Nash, to Morris A. Marks, the present owner, for $110,000.[12]

Not many family homes of those who played major roles in shaping our country's history are still standing. Even fewer remain virtually unaltered since they once lived there. The existence of two houses, side-by-side, but of different periods is, perhaps, unique. The home of Chief Justice John Marshall has all of these things and more. It is not surrounded by later buildings; its unrivalled view of the mountains is still unobstructed. Most of its out- buildings are intact including two contemporary with the original house.

In June of 1973 the present owner was notified that "Oak Hill" home of John Marshall, was entered in the National Register of Historic Places and, as such, deserved national attention.

Mr. and Mrs. Morris Marks

NOTES

Chapter One

1. Robert Carter Papers, Virginia Historical Society, quoted by Clifford Dowdey, THE VIRGINIA DYNASTIES, (Boston: Little Brown and Company, 1969), P. 360.
2. Northern Neck Grants, Book D, page 87. [Afterwards NNG: book and page]
3. NNG D: 88.
4. NNG D: 89.
5. NNG D: 90.
6. NNG E: 10, NNG E: 12.
7. NNG E: 28-31.
8. NNG D: 64
9. NNG E: 32 The survey was completed about six months before Fairfax left for England
10. NNG E: 198.
11. George Harrison Sanford King, MA.RRIAGES OF RICHMOND COUNTY, VIRGINIA, 1668-1853 (1964), p. 220.
12. Fauquier County Deed Book 5, pp. 281-285. [Afterwards, FCDB]
13. David W. Eaton, HISTORICAL ATLAS OF WESTMORELAND COUNTY, (Richmond: The Deitz Press, 1942), pp. 37-38.
14. "Germantown Revived", by Woodford B. Hackley and Benjamin C. Holtzclaw, in: THE GERMANNA RECORD Number Two, April 1962.
15. FCDB 1, pp. 70-72
16. FCDB 32 p. 70, Bond.
17. FCDB 22 pp. 424-429.
18. FCDB 2, pp. 53-59.
19. FCDB 5., pp. 48-49.

20. FCDB 5, pp. 281-285.
21. "Oak Hill, the John Marshall House", Sheet 13. Measured drawings by Thomas A. Fransioli, Jr., 1934, Virginia Historic Landmarks Commission, Richmond.
22. Thomas Tileston Waterman, THE MANSIONS OF VIRGINIA, (N. Y.: Bonanza Books, 1945), p. 308.
23. Log structures were unknown in Virginia, east of the Blue Ridge, before the Revolution.

CHAPTER TWO

1. John Marshall was noted for his indifference to dress and the Ambler girls made fun of his sloppy appearance but he was not given to coonskin caps and leggings. Leonard Baker, JOHN MARSHALL, A LIFE IN LAW, (N.Y.: Macmillian Publishing Co., Inc., 1974), p.87 et seq.
2. Fauquier County Court Minute Book, 1773-1780, p. 473. [Afterwards FCCMB]
3. Baker, op. cit., p. 83; FCDB 7 p. 533.
4. ibid., p. 84. See also: Butler, HISTORY OF KENTUCKY, p. 138.
5. FCDB 8, p. 241.
6. Frances Norton Mason, MY DEAREST POLLY (Richmond, Va.: Garrett & Massie, Inc., 1961), p. 30.
7. Stuart E. Brown, VIRGINIA BARON, (Berryville, Va.: Chesapeake Book Co., 1965), p. 187.
8. ibid., p. 199. See also: "Virginia Magazine of History and Biography," Vol. 24, p. 53.

9. Baker, op. cit., pp. 167-168.
10. Brown, op. cit., p. 199; Baker, op. cit., p. 296, et seq.
11. Mason, op cit., p. 121.

CHAPTER THREE

1. Copy filed in Chancery Suit No. 79, Fauquier County, Virginia, styled "Marshall, Jr. vs. Marshalls".
2. A copy of this letter was obtained through the courtesy of Dr. Charles F. Hobson, Director, The Papers of John Marshall, Williamsburg, VA 23187.
3. Saunders, the brick-maker, is unidentified.
4. Baker, op. cit., pp.633-635. Three former Revolutionary War officers were asked by the state to escort Lafayette, Phillip Slaughter, Gabriel Long and John Marshall. Marshall's remarks were in reply to one offered to John Marshall, "the solider, the statesman, the jurist – our country with exultation points to her son."
5. See footnote No. 1, above.
6. FCDB 15p p. 343.
7. Lee Moffett, WATER POWERED MILLS OF FAUQUIER COUNTY, VIRGINIA, (n.p., n.d.), p.69. FCDB 16, p.781 There was some doubt as to whether this was a sale or a lease, but Heniford's conveyance to Charles Fenton Mercer, FCDB 17, p. 6, proves that it was a sale.
8. W.M. Paxton, THE MARSHALL FAMILY, (Baltimore: Gateway Press, Inc., 1970; reprint of 1885 ed.) p. 195.

9. Fauquier County, Chancery Suit No. 329 styled "Marshall's Trustee vs. Marshall's Admr."
10. The place, now called "Mount Joy Farm", is west of the town of Marshall. The house was built about 1840.
11. Chancery Suit No. 329, op. cit.
12. The True Index (newspaper), Warrenton, VA., 30 June 1866.
13. FCDB 60, p. 241.
14. Chancery Suit No. 329, op. cit

CHAPTER FOUR

1. FCDB 68, p. 237.
2. ibid.
3. Photographs courtesy of George Thompson, III, great-grandson of F. Webb Maddux, Sr.
4. Unidentified newspaper clipping, ca. 1903.
5. FCDB 105, p. 436.
6. FCDB 111, p. 87.
7. Albert J. Beveridge, THE LIFE OF JOHN MARSHALL, (N.Y.: Houghton Mifflin Co., 1919), v.1, p. 56.
8. This work was done under the Works Progress Administration
9. From a program for this event in the possession of the authors. Interview with Alvin V. Baird, Jr., 21 August 1987.
10 Will Book 78, p. 301
11. FCDD 232, p. 604.

Other Heritage Books by T. Triplett Russell and John K. Gott:

An Historical Vignette of Oak Hill, Fauquier County: Home of John Marshall, Chief Justice of the United States and Native Son of Fauquier County

Fauquier County in the Revolution

The Dixon Valley, Its First 250 Years

Other Heritage Books by John K. Gott:

CD: Fauquier County, Virginia Court Records, 1776–1782

CD: Fauquier County, Virginia Deeds, 1759–1785, Volumes 1 and 2

CD: Fauquier County, Virginia Guardian Bonds, 1759–1871

CD: Fauquier County, Virginia Marriage Bonds, 1759–1854 and Marriage Returns, 1785–1848

CD: Fauquier County, Virginia

Fauquier County, Virginia Court Records, 1776–1782

Fauquier County, Virginia Deed Abstracts, 1779–1785

Fauquier County, Virginia Guardian Bonds, 1759–1871

Fauquier County, Virginia Deeds, 1759–1778

Fauquier County, Virginia Deeds, 1778–1785

Fauquier County, Virginia: Marriage Bonds (1759–1854) and Marriage Returns (1785–1848)

One Hundred Years of Cochran Lodge, 1899–1999: Cochran Lodge No. 271, A.F. & A.M., The Plains, Virginia

The Years of Anguish: Fauquier County, Virginia, 1861–1865
Emily G. Ramey and John K. Gott

Valiant Virginian: Story of Presley Neville O'Bannon, 1776–1850, to Which is Added the O'Bannon Family
Trudy J. Sundberg and John K. Gott